Janis, Jacks

# THE EVOLUTION OF DECISION MAKING
# LEARNING TO TAP INTO YOUR GENIUS

Jacques L. Austin, LPC-S, NCC

*Archdeacon Books*
Publishing Imprint of Woody Norman LLC

ARCHDEACON BOOKS

Copyright © 2015 Jacques L. Austin LPC-S, NCC
All Rights Reserved

Published in the United States of America

ISBN: 9781519211491

Book Cover Art Images
Copyright © 2015 Joycelyn Fitts

FOR JACQUELINE, JAYLIN, AND JORDAN

# Contents

Foreword .................................................................. vii

An Introduction ........................................................ ix

Preface ..................................................................... xi

Chapter 1 .................................................................... 1
    Sweetball's Story ................................................. 1

Chapter 2 .................................................................. 15
    The Sum of Your Decisions ................................ 15

Chapter 3 .................................................................. 21
    Circumstances of Your Choosing ....................... 21

Chapter 4 .................................................................. 25
    Change Your Thoughts ...................................... 25

Chapter 5 .................................................................. 29
    Evolution of Decision Making ............................ 29

Chapter 6 .................................................................. 41
    A Walk Around The Block .................................. 41

Chapter 7 .................................................................. 55
    Take a S.E.L.F., not a Selfie ................................. 55

Chapter 8 .................................................................. 63
    Discover Your Purpose ...................................... 63

Chapter 9 .................................................................. 69
    Broken Glass ....................................................... 69

Resources ................................................................. 79

**Activities Index** ..........................................................................80

**Acknowledgements** ...............................................................82

**About the Author** ...................................................................83

# Foreword

I have known Jacques Austin for over 15 years. I have observed him using the Evolution of Decision Making (EVODM) in working with the adolescent population. The use of a decision making approach is the key to helping an individual understand themselves, accept responsibility for their behavior and/or choices, improve their situation, and to discover their purpose.

For those working with individuals and/or groups in need of redirection and/or assistance in decision making I encourage you to read this book and then apply the EVODM process. I have seen this approach work and make all the difference in an adolescent moving forward and finding their purpose.

*Debra RouLaine, M.S.*
Manager
Shelby County (Alabama) Regional
Juvenile Detention Facility

# An Introduction

One of my real pleasures over the past several years has been getting to know Jacques L. Austin as a counseling leader, colleague and friend. Jacques is conscientious and hard-working, but most of all he is warm, caring and committed in his relationships with others.

Decision making is difficult for almost all of us but especially for young people and those who lack a solid foundation. Learning to understand and accept our own strengths and limitations and then being able to make decisions using these skill-sets forms the basis for sound decisions. The EVODM process that Jacques Austin has developed uses this basic principle to guide one to an orderly evaluation of the elements needed to arrive at a wise decision.

I encourage you to acquaint yourself with EVODM and use it both in your personal decision making and as you help others cope with their personal choices.

*Dr. Ervin L. (Chip) Wood*
Executive Director
Alabama Counseling Association

# Preface

This book is an accompaniment to the lecture and training on a Cognitive Behavioral Therapy approach to decision making called The Evolution of Decision Making.

Close to two decades now, in working with the 6A population (Angry, Abusive, Addicted, Adjudicated, Adult and Adolescent) I have developed a decision making approach that offers a new perspective of self-responsibility, self-control, and will forever change the way your decisions are made.

I have used this approach in counseling to help the client develop a positive perspective on his/her current circumstance, future outcomes and self-image. This approach teaches emotional responsibility and offers a guide for personal growth and fulfillment.

Decision making can be difficult. A poor decision can lead to a life filled with self-doubt, low self-esteem, or disruption from discovering our intended purpose. Our thoughts fuel our emotion. So much about our behavior is dependent upon the way we think. And what we think (self-talk) influences how we feel. For the adolescent (or the less-mature thinker) behavior is too often motivated by emotion.

It is no secret that behavior is learned. You cannot practice (behavior) what you were never taught (perspective, way of thinking). I have met an increasing number of individuals who were never taught to think positively. They are constantly bombarded with negative images of themselves, and their world. They are constantly told they are failures. These individuals become so emotionally beat down and their self-esteem so low that the words "I can't" may as well be tattooed on their foreheads. With their choices often resulting in a negative consequence, they would appear to give up on the possibility that their life could improve. They could not imagine the potential within themselves to tap into their genius. It was difficult for them to make the connection between positive thinking and positive behavior. Well, until they entered one of my sessions.

The Evolution of Decision making (EVODM), will teach you to; maintain a positive perspective of self, manage emotions responsibly, apply consequential learning, and gain confidence in future decision making. It details a self-evaluative measure that promotes improved decision making skills.

Through a series of lectures, group and individual exercises, the training teaches that each decision in life is a step toward S.E.L.F Improvement, one decision at a time.

Even when you feel as though you are moving backwards, EVODM provides a perspective on how your set-back is actually a step forward in self-discovery and purpose.

## Chapter 1
## Sweetball's Story

The journey began with Sweetball. There are still a few people who lived in the small city of Fairfield in the early 1980s who recall the name, Sweetball.

A tall, slender, athletic and attractive young man, Sweetball brandished a charming smile with an alluring wit. He was given the moniker for his finesse on the basketball court. Off the court, he was a street-smart kid raised on the west coast who now lived in a southern town not yet keen to the guile needed to survive in Los Angeles, CA. He would relish in sharing the tales of his adventures with his sister and young cousin.

He bragged of how he made guys on the basketball court look silly. "I crossed him up, faked like I was going left, brought the pill around my back. The dude's shoes still in the same spot he left them when his feet came out. I drove to the hole, BOOYA! Two hand dunk, and they all watched in amazement as I floated away from the rim landing gently on the court. They couldn't guard me because they all wanted to see what I would do. The next play I stole the ball, came back down the court, pulled up at the three…..let it fly. The net didn't say swish it cried SWEEEET!" It was difficult to tell who loved it more, the younger kids who listened with excitement and admiration, or Sweetball who spoke as if he were delivering an acceptance speech for a Hood Life Award. He held similar adoration and charm with the southern girls in the small town.

He would boast that he could charm the most prim-and-proper church ladies out of their Sunday stockings…on a Sunday. Blessed with natural athletic ability, bright and charismatic, one would assume that Sweetball's future was his to command. It was, yet what he gained through charisma, he would lose because of poor decision making.

"You can have all the talent in the world and every one of those little hussies can beat down your door, but if you don't learn to use some 'common sense' it will all go to waste," his grandmother would say. His grandmother, affectionately called Motherdear (and she made sure he enunciated), was a hardworking, educated southern woman. Motherdear's father was an entrepreneur with whom she worked as his record keeper and laborer. She credited the years of working in her father's ice house to the early onset of arthritis she struggled with in later years. While rearing seven children, she worked as a nurse for a crippled children's clinic and attended college at night. She would eventually earn a degree in education and teach until her retirement in the early 1980s, around the same time that Sweetball had come to live with her permanently.

The two shared a modest three bedroom, one bathroom home in a quiet kid friendly neighborhood with Sweetball's sister, a cousin, and their grandfather. Sweetball's grandfather was also retired, but worked nights as a sitter for an elderly gentleman who lived in an upper-class suburb often referred to as over-the-mountain.

Prior to becoming a sitter he worked many years for the booming steel industry that put Fairfield on the map.

Although Sweetball's grandparents shared the role of disciplinarian, it would be his grandfather who laid down the law. His grandfather would lay awake late at night waiting for Sweetball to come home, and then chastise him for running the streets. Sweetball thought he had outsmarted his grandfather when he decided to leave a bedroom window open to enter through after curfew. Late that evening when he returned to his grandparents' home, he quietly opened the window and perched himself halfway inside. While his head and shoulders where inside the home his lower body still hung outside the window. As he struggled to push himself in he heard a sound that sent such a fear through him he almost wet his pants. His grandfather had pulled the hammer back on the revolver he placed beside Sweetball's temple. "You should never break into a man's home, it will get you killed," his grandfather rumbled in a deep and angry tone. Albeit his grandfather was a strict disciplinarian, he was not without compassion. After Sweetball's plea to own a vehicle, his grandfather purchased an old beat-up station wagon; however, he had no idea that it would become Sweetball's mobile motel room. He would continue to show compassion when, in just a short three years later, he carried the burden of providing daily physical therapy for an arm that had become a lifeless attachment to Sweetball's left shoulder.

In the blink of an eye, Sweetball's life would collide with the consequence of poor decision making. Actually, it did not happen that fast. It was the culmination of years of poor decision making that, according to Sweetball, was the consequence of being Stuck-on-Stupid. On a winter night in 1983 his life's dreams and his family's hopes came to a sudden, shrieking, bone-crushing halt. The death of Sweetball was inevitable.

Although he had the athletic ability, he never played on the high school team. Although he had charm and charisma, he never went to a prom with the girl of his dreams, but he did become a father at age 16. Although he excelled in academics through middle school, he never graduated with his high school class. Sweetball's life was cut short long before that fateful winter night.

Sweetball's sophomore year in high school he began to run with "the wrong crowd." Certain teenagers, in the surrounding areas during that period, who longed for a sense of fun, belonging, and power, gravitated to organizations that took on Greek names but fell way short of the community service associated with true Greek membership. Organizations such as KΨA, BAQ (Beat Ass Quick) and ΣΦK were among the more popular. Sweetball chose to join the latter.

Albeit he was no saint prior to his new affiliations, this fraternal membership opened the door for like minds to ponder nefarious behaviors. Sweetball began to skip school. His fraternity meetings became opportunities to get high. His highs no longer were restricted to marijuana use; he soon graduated to painkillers and hallucinogens.

*The Evolution of Decision Making*

One evening while his sister and cousin were finishing their evening chore of cleaning the kitchen, they were startled by a light rapping at the backdoor.

The cousin opened the door and Sweetball stumbled into the arms of his sister. His eyes were glazed, his skin scratched, cut and bleeding. "Shhh," he commanded as the younger pair gasped in wonder and concern. "What happened to you?" his cousin whispered. Through deep pants and attempts to focus through the haze of whatever drug he was on, Sweetball revealed, "I saw Jesus." The kids laughed. "I was at Ya-Ya's house sitting in the living room, looking out of the window when I saw Jesus walking down the street. He stopped in front of the house and told me to come to him. He called and motioned for me to run to him. So, I ran and jumped....right through the window. When I realized Jesus wasn't there I kept running." That night Sweetball's cousin made a mental note: "Whatever he is high on right now, **never do that drug**."

Sweetball soon began to break into cars and snatch purses from unsuspecting mall shoppers. He would have constant verbal bouts with his grandparents about his late night adventures, poor school attendance, choice of friends, and disregard for the law. Soon the discipline handed out by his grandparents became ineffective, the time spent with his peers became more important, and run-ins with the local police became too frequent. By age 18 it was decided he would attain a GED then join the military. His grandfather insisted he needed to learn structure and self-

Jacques L. Austin

discipline, but primarily he needed to get out of Fairfield where the Police knew him by his deeds.

Sweetball's excursion into the military was a short reprieve for the city of Fairfield, his grandparents and his cousin. The young cousin had moved into Sweetball's bedroom only to be booted back onto the living room sofa when he returned. Sweetball's young cousin was both happy and saddened by his return. Happy because he looked up to his older cousin, and saddened because Sweetball was the source of his torment.

One evening Sweetball convinced his cousin to climb atop the roof of his station wagon. The young and impressionable cousin imagined he was Colonel Steve Austin (The Six-Million Dollar Man) as he made the climb down from the porch bannister then onto the roof the vehicle. He never suspected Sweetball would hop behind the wheel and barrel off through the dimly lit streets of Fairfield. He held on for dear life as his body flung from either side of the luggage rack. Sweetball floored the vehicle as he drove beside the elementary school. The street alongside of it lead to a double hill that acted as a ramp for any car, bike, or moped that traveled faster than 25mph. The station wagon became airborne, and so was his cousin; however, his bionic grip never loosened. As the wheels and undercarriage hit the ground so did his chin onto the roof of the car. When they returned to their grandparents' home, Motherdear asked the cousin "What happened to your chin," he replied, "Fell down while running outside."

The cousin knew the torture that Sweetball would unleash if he told the truth. The basketball Sweetball used to establish his dominance on the court? It belonged to his cousin. The only Christmas gift he received that year, yet was never given the opportunity to play with it. His cousin recalled feeling sore for a month from the sharp blows delivered by Sweetball for telling Motherdear about that basketball. It was one of several possessions that Sweetball would claim as his. Yes, his return from the military was both welcomed and jeered.

During Sweetball's absence while in the military a few of his close friends acquired motorcycles. They welcomed him back to the fold by encouraging that he should get one as well. Of all the decisions his grandmother attempted to dissuade Sweetball from making, this was the one she pleaded with him the most. Sweetball had returned with a larger sum of money than one would expect after barely completing basic training. No one questioned it. Sweetball simply advised his grandmother, "It's my money and I'll do what I want with it."

They could hear it before they saw it. The rumble of its engine vibrated along the side of the house as Sweetball rode up the driveway toward the garage. Sweetball's cousin and sister burst out of the backdoor and into the backyard, and there it was....Kawasaki 750 Turbo, red on black...a beast of a machine, or a pocket-rocket, their grandfather used to call it. The sunlight shimmered across the chrome. Sweetball revved the engine and the younger kids jumped back in excitement. His sister yelled, "I wanna ride, I wanna ride." While his cousin, who had learned better than to ride in or on anything that Sweetball was driving, stepped back even further. As Sweetball left the driveway with his sister in-tow, his cousin entered the house. Motherdear was perched on her stool at the kitchen sink. He noticed the sadness on her face and the sorrow in her eyes. It was as if she knew what lay ahead.

It was not long before Sweetball had fallen back into old habits. Only difference now, he straddled a vehicle that allowed for a quick getaway. Sweetball's cousin would learn of his late-night exploits through conversations in the halls of his high school. "I saw your cousin last night," said a classmate. "Where?" asked the cousin. "He was on his bike, with Fairfield [Police] behind him. I cut the police off before I realized they were chasing him. Did they catch him?" The cousin noticed a twinkle of admiration and hope in the eye of his classmate. She was actually proud of her gesture of assistance, as if Sweetball would notice and thank her personally with an eternal affection for her. "No, they did not catch him, thanks to you I guess. He made it home last night or this morning rather," said the bewildered cousin. The classmate sighed in relief and exhilaration as she panted, "Will you tell him it was me in the red Escort?"

A turbo charged motorcycle made criminal mischief a lot easier, or so Sweetball thought. On one heist he did not expect the police would be patrolling the mall area so heavily. The mall straddled the border of neighboring cities; therefore, the ensuing chase involved officers from both Fairfield and Midfield. He first led the chase through the streets of Midfield, winding and twisting his way as best he could through the unfamiliar neighborhood. He knew once he crossed the super highway and got back into Fairfield he could lose them. As he barreled along the cross street with the super highway ahead and the police matching every move, he pondered if he would be able to slow down before crossing or take a chance that there may not be any cross traffic. Slowing down would lead to the possibility of getting caught. He dropped the bike into the next lower gear and gunned it. He noticed the blur of a church across his left shoulder and in that moment he whispered a prayer, "God be with me." You see, long before he became Sweetball he was taught to fear the Lord. His grandmother made sure he knew of God's grace, mercy and the resurrection of His son Jesus Christ.

The red on black Kawasaki took flight as he crested the hill intersecting the busy highway. Sweetball's prayer was answered. As he landed on the far side of the highway he had to travel against oncoming traffic before veering left and escaping into familiar territory, while the officers in pursuit were met with cross traffic. This bought him only seconds. Fairfield police, already on alert were speeding toward his direction. The opposing forces met at a five-way intersection. It seemed as though Sweetball was finally corralled. Holding the front brake and gunning the throttle, his tires howled as he left a cloud of burnt rubber and vanished into an alley along-side a corner gas station. In spite of his determination to escape, it seemed as though the entire police force from both cities were intent that this would be their last day chasing Sweetball.

He sped through the projects behind the college. He thought that with just a little more speed he could cut through the side streets and get to his grandmother's house long before the police were even within four blocks, but there were more of them, and they seemed to counter his every move. In the midst of all this turmoil, while in the center of a storm of police cars and adrenaline, he heard a soft voice whisper to him saying, "Mama's house."

"Mama" was the title given to Motherdear's mother, Sweetball's great-grandmother. She lived in a suburb twenty minutes outside of Fairfield. Sweetball made it there in five. Once he hit the slab of concrete, on I-20 East, the pursuing lights and sirens silenced in the distance. Sweetball with chin touching the gas tank, gripped his bike tightly as he swerved through traffic. His knee nearly scrapped the pavement as he leaned into the hard right turn off of I-20 onto I-65. Mama's house was now only three exits away. Darkness had fallen as he exited the highway and cruised to Motherdear's childhood home. He quickly drove around back, covered the bike with an old rug and walked around front. He grinned as he sat on Mama's porch swing, looking at a police station which sat within eyesight. He whispered, "Not today boys, not today." But the day did come.

The day that Sweetball's reign of merriment came to a grinding, metal crushing, and bone splintering end happened in Ensley, another city that neighbors Fairfield. True to form, Sweetball made another decision that would result in his running from the authorities. While speeding down the avenue, head down, self-assured and confident in the ability of his pocket-rocket to outrun his pursuer, Sweetball turned to look back and did not notice the car pulling out in front of him. He was going too fast to avoid the metal wall that waited. He laid the bike down as both he and all 750 horses slid underneath. He was trampled, and left mangled as the car continued in its path with Sweetball twisting between its belly and the pavement.

Sweetball remained comatose for five weeks at Lloyd Nolan Hospital. The doctors' early prognosis was death. But, Sweetball had a praying grandmother and they soon reported permanent brain damage, a slim possibility of ever walking again, a broken left arm, crushed left shoulder and internal injuries. While he lay in the hospital hooked to hoses, and ventilators he was visited by several friends and relatives. Nights of prayer and vigilance turned into mornings of hope and faith. Sweetball eventually left the hospital but not the hospital bed. The two were moved into the small bedroom shared with his cousin.

The entire family took responsibility for feeding and caring for him. Sweetball's grandfather and cousin shared in the physical labor of moving him, sitting him on the side of the bed, bathing him, and changing his diaper. His cousin bore the sounds of his waking nightmares, moments of sorrow and regret filled with cries for a life lost. Time passed, the trachea site healed and Sweetball learned to walk without assistance; however, his left arm remained permanently disabled and disfigured. He would carry his left hand to aid in balance as he walked or trotted, as a reminder of a life that was forever changed.

Sweetball's grandfather died five years after his accident. His cousin, home from the military to attend the funeral, sat beside Sweetball in their small bedroom. The two recalled their lives together with their grandfather and the challenge of being reared by such a staunch disciplinarian. The cousin asked, "Sweetball, why couldn't you just listen to what he was telling you? He wasn't telling either of us anything wrong or requiring us to do anything that was unfair. He wanted the best for you and did all but give you everything you asked for. I don't understand it, how did you go so far left?"

Sweetball sat up, exhaled slowly and looked into his cousin's eyes and replied, "……. Everything I did, I knew better than to do. I wanted to have fun and really could care less about what everyone was telling me not to do. I can sit here now and say I wish that I had listened. I heard him, I still hear him but you're right. I wasn't listening. I know the difference now. I wish that I had considered how my choices then, would affect my future. They both tried, Granddaddy and Motherdear tried to keep me from destroying myself. They tried to save me from myself. The things I put them through, when they were only trying to help me. On a lot of occasions they did save me, but it would only last so long because I was simply stuck-on-stupid……. Sweetball……was stuck-on-stupid and that's why he died in a motorcycle accident five years ago."

He turned toward the mirror, peering at his reflection, and continued to speak, "Sweetball is dead, and I want to be known by my given name only, Errol. Errol lives…… Sweetball had his chance and now Errol is alive to tell the story."

"Maybe my story will help someone. I hope what I went through will be a tale of caution to some young kid who is in a similar circumstance. I don't know. What I do know is that I'm going to tell anyone who will listen. I wasn't supposed to be here, but God had a plan for me. I have a purpose and God's grace allowed me to be here to share my story of His love, mercy, and the gift of his only begotten Son, Jesus Christ."

## Chapter 2
## The Sum of Your Decisions

Fast forward thirty-five years. Life experience, formal education, and practice in the counseling field inspired an approach to decision making.

A client in the court diversion program T.A.S.C (Treatment Alternative to Street Crimes) commented after participating in a Cognitive Skills Group, "If someone had told me what you're telling me today when I was 17 years old, I wouldn't be in this situation." That attestation from a 52 year old, angry, addicted, adjudicated, adult stayed with me, and fueled this approach to decision making and the effect poor decision making has on self-esteem. After leaving T.A.S.C., I began to work full-time with adolescents in an attempt to reach a younger population with an approach that speaks directly to them. Not above, around or beneath, but to engage them in what they call 'real-talk.'

One morning my two-year old daughter stood in front of the mirror in only her pull-up and flexed her muscles. She smiled and laughed as she clinched her fist and tightened her stomach and gave her best Wonder Woman pose. As I watched her amazement and joy with the reflection of herself, I could not help but wonder if, in 50 years as she poses nearly naked in the mirror, will she express the same joy with what she sees?

Along this same time line, a family member asked my advice on one of life's challenges he was facing. As I pointed out his responsibility in the resulting consequence he became agitated, angry and reluctant to accept the perspective. Rather than acknowledge any responsibility for his circumstance, he found the widely accepted course of action of ==blaming someone or something else== to be a better explanation.

I contemplated the two scenarios and resigned myself to the fact that looking into a mirror can be difficult at times; however, when someone else is holding the mirror and points out what is seen, well, it becomes difficult to accept.

When the time comes for a sincere reflection into your life's mirror, will you like what you see? How easy is it to accept the advice of those who know what your life reflects? Your choices and their consequences will determine if your life's reflection is one you're proud of or a reflection that you're ashamed to reveal.

Therapists working with the 6A population initially hold the mirror and identify what is there. That is just one step. The next is to find methods and techniques of coping, adjusting, letting go, and/or building upon skills you already possess. Self-awareness (learning to hold your own mirror), emotional responsibility (acknowledging what is reflected), self-management (affectively applying adjustments for improvement), and the self-confidence to improve decision making are all key characteristics taught in the EVODM approach.

*(you get what you put in) –*

*The Evolution of Decision Making*

Common characteristics observed among the 6A population include:

- Poor decision making
- Lack of emotional responsibility
- Low self-esteem
- Poor consequential learning

*Life is a sum of all your choices*
Albert Camus

There comes a point in everyone's life when they must take a self-reflective look into their life's mirror. Of course, taking that look at age two is not quite the same perspective as at age fifty-two.

It is the sum of the decisions made within that time period that determines whether you experience feelings of accomplishment or emotions of despair.

Imagine when that moment of self-reflection comes and you find yourself waking on a beautiful fall morning. As you rise to sit on the side of your king-sized bed after a night of resting peacefully, you gaze out of your bedroom window and see the acres of land that you own, placed along-side a pristine lake. The aroma of apple-wood bacon frying in your kitchen, the sound of children rustling through your dream home, and the comfort of your slippers await you as you stand to start your day.

Jacques L. Austin

After you dress and prepare to go to a job you enjoy, you kiss your spouse and leave to get into that automobile you have always dreamed of owning. As you adjust the rearview mirror and catch a reflection of yourself, you think back on all the decisions throughout your life that have led you to this moment. A self-reflective moment may come at a dinner in your honor or over a quiet table with your elderly parents holding your hand, looking into your eyes as they acknowledge their pride and joy for you.

That moment may come as you watch your child receive his or her diploma or degree while you recall the challenges you overcame to bring reality to the goal. A strong sense of achievement, gratitude, self-confidence, and excitement overcomes you, because you are confident in your ability to take on life's next challenges.

Now, imagine when that moment of self-reflection comes and it finds you waking one morning, sitting on a two-inch-thick twin mattress atop a metal frame in a concrete cell shared with three others who care less for your life than a cockroach on the floor. You rise slowly, grimacing from the pain in your back and neck from a night of restless sleep. Then, like an open hand slap the stench of body odor and the funk from the morning bowel movement your cellmate is currently taking hits your senses. You turn and gaze between the bars of your windowless cell and see many more caged just as you are.

*The Evolution of Decision Making*

As you face your reflection in the aluminum sheet placed on the wall above a rusted-out sink, you think back on all the decisions throughout your life that have lead you to this moment. A self-reflective moment may come as you are walking into a shell of the home once filled with love prior to the divorce, or when you have to toil daily at a job you hate for a boss you despise. It may come when a lifetime of wrongdoing is finally brought to light in the realm of public opinion. Then, you are overcome with a burdening sense of failure, blame, despair, depression, guilt, and very little self-confidence in your ability to take on life's challenges successfully.

Of the two scenarios given, which individual is likely to make the comment, "Life sucks?"

That statement is often expressed among the 6A. I always replied, "Life does not suck, only some of the choices that are made suck. Your capacity for consequential learning can determine if you will have a life of happiness or one of misery."

*Every man has his challenges.*
*Whether he overcomes or comes-undone*
*Is a matter of his choosing.*

2-27-23 - Chp. 3 - Circumstance -

In 4th grade after school I walked to an elderly ladies house close to school until my mom picked me up. She was a Jehovah's Witness. She taught me about how to live for Christ, I learned from her and her family by witnessing them what a Christ based life looked like, following the 10 commandments. I remember the picture of the 10 commandments and of Jesus at the last Supper paintings in her house.

Later in the fall a new girl came to our class, Tracy. She lived on the same street of the family and lady who watched me. Tracy and I became fast friends and now walked home together every afternoon. After I did my homework, she would let Tracy and I walk to the corner store together. Sometimes she gave me $$ from her coin purse to bring her back a few groceries, Tracy always had money and she was allowed to buy candy with left overs. I knew I was expected to buy what was on the list and return the change. Tracy would dare me to buy something extra at first, but then when I didn't she dared me to take something. After a few weeks of me doing neither - Tracy started calling me names and putting me down and telling kids at school I wasn't a good friend and I never took her advice. After awhile she would show me all the stuff she took while I was paying and how easy it was and I was stupid -

After some thought - I decided that since I knew where the ladies coin purse was kept I would just take a few extra coins - instead of taking it from store. All the while knowing it was wrong to steal. I got more and more greedy and one day took an entire $1.00 - the lady noticed.

She sat me down and told me she knew all those months I was taking change from her coin purse - she thought I would confess or stop - knowing it was wrong as we talked about the commandments daily and why we don't take from others - we ask, she said - she would of given me coins on occ if I asked - but stealing a $1.00 - I had to tell my parents what I had been doing all these months, because I had not been a good guest in her home and broken her trust. I lied to my parents and told them I had only done a few times and for only small coins out of her purse. She asked my mom the next day and my mom told her what I had told my parents. The lady sat me down and told me by lieing I had broken another commandment and that these lies and stealing would eventually catch up to me, if I didn't undo the actions and decisions

*[Handwritten at top of page:]* was making. They did - Tracy became my bully and told everyone at school and her parents and the lady who watched me and her family - That it was my idea, and I wanted her to steel things from store, and told her how to take coins from her parents. She continued to bully me on our walks and started to physically assault me the last week of school. She told everyone she did that b/c she was putting me in my place for steeling $$ from old elderly women and steeling from the corner store.

## Chapter 3
### Circumstances of Your Choosing

*Many of life's circumstances are created by three basic choices:*
*The Disciplines <u>you choose</u> to keep*
*The People <u>you choose</u> to be with*
*The Laws <u>you choose</u> to obey*

Recall any circumstance in your life, either good or bad. How much of it was created by either one or all of the choices listed above?

Do you rise each morning with a genuine excitement about what you can accomplish that day, or are you one to cling to your pillow for twenty minutes more of sleep, dreading to leave the comfort of your bed?

*Cling to bed*

Are you the smartest one in your group of peers? Have you or anyone close to you questioned why you choose to associate with a certain friend? Have you found yourself with the wrong person, at the wrong place at the wrong time? *Yes,*

Are you one to eat whatever is quick to get your hands on, or are you more cautious about what you choose to include in your diet? *Cautious*

Are you one to engage in some form of physical activity daily, or do you gorge until you are stuffed and plop onto the couch where burping and passing gas are your only forms of physical activity?

*[Handwritten at bottom:]* I learned a hard lesson, the next year I didn't get to go to the woman's house anymore I had to walk home - a mile in a half each day. I did apologize to the woman and her family - but I had 21 broken their trust and worse I had broken the commandments in which they strived to teach me and they lived by. They loved me, but I couldn't stay at their home anymore.

Jacques L. Austin

Have you developed a work ethic that allows you to earn and progress in society, or do you look at those who are successful with jealousy and envy because you think they do not deserve what they have?

As a therapist, and going into the homes of many families, I have seen that many basic disciplines are not taught to children. Wake up early, eat healthy, basic hygiene, respect your elders, respect others' property, ask nicely, say thank you and please, hard work pays off, diligence, patience, integrity, and "you are not going to always get what you want," are all lessons that start at home. My grandfather used to say,

> "*You can let me teach you or you can let the world teach you. Only thing about the world teaching you......
> it can be a hard and unforgiving lesson to learn.*"

Who sent you here? Who is responsible for your current circumstance?

These are questions I posed to the 6A. More often than not, the response would be, "The Judge made me come" or "My probation officer said I had to do this to stay out of jail." I have even heard "If she had not pissed me off, I would not have had to hit her." In each of the responses someone else is blamed for their circumstance.

> *To be a man is, precisely, to be responsible.*
> Antoine de Saint-Exupery

# Responsibility = Choice + Consequence

When another person is blamed for a consequence that you have to endure, that means you are waiting for that person to change in order for your circumstance to improve. What happens when the person being blamed never changes? Then your circumstance will never improve. Look within for change. Look at S.E.L.F., for improvement to your circumstance, and for improvement in your life.

CHANGE STARTS WITH SELF

What can YOU do differently that will improve YOUR circumstance?

Start with THINKING differently. There is a connection between what you are thinking, how you are feeling and how you choose to behave. The following chart illustrates the first skill shared with the 1A population, the angry client.

*— Core Beliefs —*  *2/28/23*

# Chapter 4
## Change Your Thoughts

*Change your thoughts and you change your world*
Norman Vincent Peale

**Illustration 1**

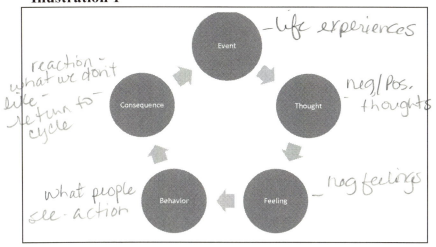

*— life experiences*
*neg/Pos. thoughts*
*— neg feelings*
*what people see - action*
*reaction - what we don't like - return to cycle*

The cycle above begins with an event.

EVENT – Something happens that you do not like or were not expecting. In other words "LIFE" happens. Although events are often beyond your control, you do have control over how you choose to interpret and react to those events.

THOUGHT – The internal message, your personal interpretation of the event (self-talk). This is the most critical point of the cycle. Your thoughts determine how you feel. Thoughts such as, "I'm going to fail, I'll never be good enough" will elicit a very different emotion than the thought, "I can do this; I'm going to be great."

**FEELINGS** – Emotions such as Anger, Guilt, Joy, Love, Hate, Grief, or feeling Depressed, are derived from the thoughts about the event. If an event caused the emotion, then everyone would share the same emotions about the same events; but everyone does not. Different perceptions (thoughts) will produce different feelings about the event.

**BEHAVIOR** – Actions, what you do. You will not be arrested for feeling like you want to rob a bank. You will not be arrested if you think about robbing a bank. It is not until you take actions to actually rob a bank that you begin to commit a crime.

**CONSEQUENCE** – For every action, there is a reaction. The result, both negative and positive, of a behavior is its consequence.

The Adolescent or an immature decision-maker will often allow an emotion to dictate the behavior. When that happens, it will often result in a negative consequence. So, what happens when the consequence is something you don't like or were not expecting? Then you are thrust back into that cycle shown in Illustration 1.

The only way to break the cycle and allow for a different, more positive consequence would be to change your thoughts. Changing your thoughts will open the option for choosing a different behavior. As long as the thought process is limited to producing negative emotions, the resulting behaviors will produce negative consequences.

*The Evolution of Decision Making*

Activity #1
**PERSPECTIVE**
**(Identifying your automatic thoughts)**

Years ago I compiled a list of positive quotes to display in the office. It was used as a discussion guide for the question, "How do I change my thinking?" I would point to the poster and process with the client how these statements may influence their perspective on positive thinking. I encourage you to incorporate these into your daily mantras.

POSITIVE THINKING LEADS TO POSITIVE BEHAVIORS

*Our minds can shape the way a thing will be because we act according to our expectations.* -F. Fellini

*The happiness of your life depends upon the quality of your thoughts…. Take care that you entertain no notion unsuitable to virtue and reasonable nature.* -M. Aurelius

*All that we are is the result of what we have thought. The mind is everything. What we think we become.* –Buddha

*Think you can, or think you can't; either way you will be right.* –H. Fonda

*Thoughts drift - are they neg ??*

*Our best friends and our worst enemies are our thoughts. A thought can do us more good than a doctor or a banker or a faithful friend. It can also do us more harm than a brick or a bullet.* –Dr. F. Crane

*No one can defeat us unless we first defeat ourselves.* –D. D. Eisenhower

Jacques L. Austin

*I am happy and content because I think I am.* – A. R. Lesage

*The world is like a mirror; frown at it, and it frowns at you. Smile and it smiles, too.* –H. Samuels

*We can accomplish almost anything within our ability if we but THINK that we can.* –G. M. Adams

Find positive affirmations from anyplace you can. Write them down, carry it with you to pull out and read anytime negative thoughts creep into your mind. Place them through-out your home to read as you carry out your daily chores. Just as you nourish your bodies with healthy food, you must nourish your mind with positive thinking.

Activity #2
**QUOTES FOR LEARNING TO THINK DIFFERENTLY**

## Chapter 5
## Evolution of Decision Making

As a living creature you evolve; you grow gradually becoming better than you were the day before. From the moment of birth you grow and develop physically. As you encounter various people you grow socially. As you experience life's trials you grow emotionally. Throughout all of this you are faced with times of decision, from the infant learning not to touch the hot stove, to the adult preparing for retirement. You grow from a state of not knowing to fully understanding and using that knowledge in your daily decisions.

Of course, as children there are many things of which you are ignorant, and as children you are given a reprieve. But as adults, ignorance is a state you are expected to have moved beyond. In certain cases ignorance is understood. For example: A warm summer day in a park filled with people enjoying the sun. An infant dashes across the grass with a parent in pursuit. The infant dressed in only a diaper which is loose and soggy snatches the garment away and laughs joyfully as onlookers join in the child's merriment at the sight of the parent's embarrassment. No harm, no foul. It was a child who, everyone knows, does not know any better.

In contrast, if an adult were to dash naked across that same lawn on this warm summer day of course many would be laughing, but it would be the police and not his parent in hot pursuit. Why? Because the adult is expected to know better.

Many cannot or do not know how to lay tile. But all are not totally ignorant of the skill. A person could study, learn, practice and become proficient in the art. It is possible to gain intelligence.

Knowing that you can remove yourself from a state of ignorance and into one of intelligence nurtures a positive perspective. You must first accept the personal responsibility when a dumb or stupid decision is made. Learn from it and make every effort to prevent the behavior from being repeated. Once you have learned to make intelligent choices, simply by increasing your awareness, then you have made an evolving step in maturity.

**Activity #3 A Children's Story**
In this exercise story telling is used to illustrate the influences and effects of poor decision making.

The Evolution of Decision Making (EVODM) identifies seven decision types. It is critical to identify specific behaviors/emotions and label them correctly. If we fail to do so, we tend to call something it actually is not.

New clients attending anger management groups would often wrongly label an emotion. Having not gained the awareness of distinguishing frustration from anger, or sadness from depression, clients would put themselves in a category of a more intense emotion. With work (on increased awareness and self-control) they learned that frustration and sadness are less intensive emotions and easier to control than anger or depression.

*The Evolution of Decision Making*

The same concept is applied in this approach to decision making. Understanding the decision types and applying consequential learning are building blocks to improved decision making.

### 7 Decision Types
The first four result in a positive consequence. The consequence and the effort prior to making the decision will determine the decision type.

GENIUS – A decision of extraordinary intellect and creative power.

Think of someone you consider to be a genius. Someone who has created, developed, or imagined beyond what others of their time have done. James Naismith, Otis Boykin, George Washington Carver, Nikola Tesla, Elijah McCoy, Sarah E Goode, Katherine Burr Blodgett, Lonnie Johnson, Joy Mangano, Margaret Knight, Patricia Bath, all were able to tap into their genius. Ordinary individuals who discovered their ability to apply, imagine, and conceive things in such a way that was very different from what was previously done. Genius may come as a result of years of practicing intelligence or simply through an innate ability to imagine and create.

My grandfather shared with me the story of a newspaper boy who, while on his route, came upon a group of emergency personnel and traffic engineers toiling to assist a semi-truck which had become stuck under a low bridge. The engineers thought of several options but none would work without destroying the bridge and interrupting the flow of traffic. The lowly newspaper carrier suggested "let the air out of the tires and pull it through." "Genius," the engineers shouted! No one else thought of that. The moral to the story my grandfather grumbled, is "genius is simply being able to see the solution to a problem from a perspective no one had imagined before, and it doesn't require a degree or that you be a rocket scientist. It only takes a creative mind."

INTELLIGENCE – Showing sound judgment and rationality, gained through formal training or years of experience.

An intelligent decision is made when it is apparent that research was done, questions asked and answered, and awareness increased prior to deciding upon an action. Teachers, professors, instructors or anyone who knows their topic well enough to advise or instruct others, demonstrate intelligence. The value of education is immeasurable. Education is the gateway to awareness, success, and freedom. Education does not only come from sitting in a classroom and testing on previously-lectured material to receive a document attesting to your ability to learn. It is gained through experimenting, failing, and trying again. It's gained through working alongside a mentor, practicing a trade, skill, or talent and honing that ability to a point of near perfection.

Intelligence is gained when Consequential Learning is consistently applied and the individual uses this

## The Evolution of Decision Making

knowledge to perfect the trial. Most often through this procedure, genius is tapped. When intelligence is consistently practiced, genius can be attained.

You have the ability to tap into your genius. It may not be in the computer industry, or the medical field, but genius can occur where ever you practice intelligence.

SMART – Sharp quick thought, gained through personal or shared experiences. An individual learns from the past mistakes made by self and others. Consequential Learning is most apparent in this decision type.

A smart decision is best illustrated when you observe the play of a quarterback (QB). For example: It is third down and 12 yards to go for a first down. It is a passing down. The QB takes the snap, drops back, searches for his number one pass option, and throws what he thinks will be a first down, but the defense's safety, reading the QB's eyes, drops underneath just in time to intercept the post pattern throw. When the QB returns to play on his next offensive possession he remembers the previous interception. He studies the defense, recognizes their formation against the play called in the huddle. He yells an audible, knowing the safety will try to cut underneath again, and calls for a Slugo pattern (fake slant route, sprint up-field for deep pass)........BOOM! Touchdown! That was smart.

Smart decisions occur in the moment. Once they become ingrained as part of your daily process, making smart decisions becomes intuitive. Great success can be attained by practicing smart decision making.

BRIGHT – Common sense is used. Being observant, noticing the obvious.

Driving along a road, the driver comes upon flashing red lights on either side of her. In front are a set of iron rails crossing the road. A red and white striped pole begins to descend in front of the driver, blocking advancement. A loud blast echoes in the distance along with the sound of a huge metal beast moving along the track in her direction. It does not take a genius to recognize that a train is coming. It does not require a person to be smart, either. It only requires that a person pay attention to the obvious and does not cross the tracks. In this example, ignoring the obvious and not making a bright decision can turn deadly.

The following three decisions typically result in a negative consequence. The consequence and lack of effort prior to making the decision determines the type.

DUMB – Decisions made resulting in a negative consequence, but a lesson is learned. Actions are taken to prevent repeating the same behavior.

I recall an individual who thought it would be a good idea to place hundreds of pounds of plywood onto the roof of his four-door sedan. As he drove away, all of the wood shifted toward the rear collapsing the vehicle, causing it to drag and making it impossible to drive. Apparently it turned out to be a dumb decision. Hopefully he learned, consequentially, that attempting to tie that much wood to the roof of a car was a dumb decision. The individual will probably look back on the decision as the day he did something really dumb, but the second part to the story will be telling what he did differently now, having learned from the consequence.

What may have turned out to be a dumb decision does not always start out as such. A person may consider trying something they have never tried before; however, the intelligent thing to do would be to gather more information before deciding on an action. If it is something already known to result in a negative consequence, and yet the same behavior is repeated, well, that is just stupid.

<u>STUPID</u> – Repeat a behavior already known to result in a negative consequence. Have the knowledge or experience yet choose to repeat the same action.

Imagine a bird attempting to fly through a window. It repeatedly hits the glass attempting to get to or get away from something. Stupidity occurs when an action known to result in a negative consequence is repeated. You are not a bird-brained individual who beats your head repeatedly against an immovable object hoping for a new outcome to the same behavior. In short, you're not STUPID. When a negative consequence results from a decision, a different course of action must be taken.

"If you continue to do what you've always done, then you will continue to get what you have always gotten."
The damage to an individual's self-esteem and confidence in repeatedly making bad decisions can be catastrophic.

Individuals who are STUCK-ON-STUPID usually are what society has labeled as "Repeat Offenders." A consequence of being STUCK-ON-STUPID is very little self-confidence in the ability to turn life around or "fix stupid." These individuals have allowed years of poor decision making to become the definition of who they are. Often telling themselves (sclf-talk), "I always mess up, what's the point of trying; I can never get it right." They begin to shift blame. No longer looking within as a source for improvement, everyone else becomes the reason for their circumstance. They spend time in their circumstance believing and waiting for someone besides themselves to change.

<u>IGNORANT</u> – The lack of knowledge or experience. Unaware / Uninformed.

From birth until an individual becomes aware, they remain ignorant. They have not yet had the experience nor have been informed. Stupidity is often confused with ignorance. Someone will do something 'off-the-wall' and another who observed the behavior will say, "Man, you ignant," as it is pronounced in southern slang.

A toddler frolicking through the park with only a soggy diaper in his hand is ignorant of the social faux pas of running nude in public places. The adult running naked across the sports field is not "ignant." His chosen behavior is stupid because he does know better. To remain ignorant is a choice. Choosing to not become informed or aware impedes growth, maturity, and the likelihood for success. Stubbornness, pride, or ego are often the impeding characteristics.

Illustration 2

## Evolution of decision-making

- Genius
- Intelligent
- Smart
- Bright
- Dumb
- Stupid
- Ignorant

- As we grow in knowledge and understanding we evolve from a state of ignorance into a state of awareness.

- As our awareness and experiences are increased we become capable of making better decisions.

- Our decisions, however, can vary with the situation. Making an intelligent decision one minute, then a dumb decision the moment we enter a different environment.

- Even worse, there are those who repeat decisions known to result in a negative consequence no matter the environment.

Just as you mature physically and emotionally into adulthood, you are also expected to mature in your decision making. Becoming a mature decision-maker means you no longer make the same dumb or stupid decision you might have made at ages 14 or 21.

As you experience various situations and familiar scenarios you must use that information to guide your future choices. Mature decision-makers are no longer guided purely by emotion. They use their power to choose, for the purpose of improving their lives.

It is possible, however, to make an intelligent decision in a specific environment, and then walk into the next room and make the most stupid decision of your life. For example: some college and professional football players are smart or even intelligent decision-makers on the football field. As soon as they take off their pads and enter the general public some become Stuck-on-Stupid. When this happens, it is obvious that Consequential Learning, in that environment, has not occurred.

Consequential Learning must occur before a person is able to evolve from a poor decision-maker into a mature decision-maker.

**Consequential Learning** is the process in which future decisions are based on past outcomes. The increased awareness of possible outcomes resulting from personal experiences and/or the known experiences of others is used to guide future decision making. In short:

ONCE YOU LEARN BETTER, THEN DO BETTER.

How does one TAP INTO THEIR GENIUS? The answer is simple.

DON'T BECOME STUCK-ON-STUPID!
PRACTICE INTELLIGENCE!

Mature-thinkers are not expected to never make a dumb or stupid decision; however, they will not continuously repeat a behavior known to result in a negative consequence.

As stated in the previous illustration, "As our awareness and experiences are increased we become capable of making better decisions."

Although there are individuals who do not aspire to be the very best among their peers, most typically do not strive to be the very worst either. Improving the types of decisions consistently made brings self-confidence, self-responsibility, self-respect, and courage to meet the challenges life brings with it.

## **Activity #4 EVODM**

*The Man who views the world at 50 the same as he did at 20, has wasted 30 years of his life.*
-Muhammed Ali

## Chapter 6
## A Walk Around The Block

It was a gorgeous spring Friday at The Adolescent Treatment Program. The program was a day-treatment facility that served at-risk adolescents in 7th through 11$^{th}$ grades. It was a place of second or in some cases third chances. I was a Counselor and in my sixth year with the program.

It was housed in a two-story brick building nestled in a quiet neighborhood. It sat less than 100 yards from a vacant shell of an old cotton mill. Between the two structures lay a railroad line that provided daily scheduled distractions for the students. Whenever the metal beast roared down its tracks it caused vibrations to an aged building that shed pieces of its self with each passing. On this beautiful day I stood in the foyer awaiting the arrival of a parent. An earlier altercation with a student prompted the ensuing meeting.

Students were not allowed to leave the property during the course of the day. During their group-counseling period, the last period of the day, students were allowed to participate in structured, supervised activities. Fridays were free days. Only under supervision of a staff member could the students leave the dreary confines of the building. Well, except for those who had lost the privilege due to their misbehavior over the past week. Students who had earned the privilege to go outside could play basketball, football, board games or socialize with their peers as they took a walk around the block. The "no-breakers," those without the privilege, would remain in the building to continue course-work.

It was a welcoming spring day after several weeks of a rainy, cloudy and cold winter. I must admit it was such a splendid day that even I longed to be among those going outdoors to bask in the beauty of spring; however, the obligation to supervise the no-breakers had fallen upon me that week. The no-break room sat deep within the belly of the building. It was often cold, noiseless and without windows. For some students, the time in the no-break room supplied an extra hour to complete valuable course work without distraction. For others it was an opportunity to put their defiance on full display.

The level of focus and self-discipline required to sit quietly, study, and not fall asleep for 50 minutes may as well have been the same amount of effort and concentration needed to survive eight weeks of Army Ranger training. During my tenure there I had seen everything from fights, screaming fits, crying, and yelling occur within the first five minutes of the no-break period. On this day, one particular student's lack of self-control and defiance of authority would collide with my obligation to maintain order.

Many of the students were referred to the program by the juvenile probation office as behavior referrals. Nelson, an academic referral, was referred by the County School System. Meaning, his behaviors in the classroom and at home lead to an academic decline. Three months earlier

## The Evolution of Decision Making

during the intake evaluation with Nelson and his father, the battle weary parent expressed his frustration with his only son. "I'm done. I've tried everything I know to try and get through to him, but you can't tell him anything. He's hard-headed, won't listen and now he has fallen behind in school.

"He is supposed be in the 12th grade next school year but he's not even finished the 10th grade. He's not a dumb kid, he can do the work, he's just choosing not to . . . becoming more defiant at home and whupping him doesn't work. I want to choke some sense into him, or the stupidity out, whichever comes first. He has brought me to that point. If this program doesn't work, then he can go get a GED and get the hell out of my house. Because I'm done," the parent lamented with conviction and heartache as he held back tears.

Nelson's first few weeks at *The Program* were ideal. He worked hard in class. His counseling sessions during this period were productive. I began to see the child in the body of an adolescent with the physique of a linebacker. In each session he progressively shared the thoughts and feelings that motivated his past behaviors. He soon became one of the few students to earn extra privileges.

Because of Nelson's consistent days of stellar behavior and academic progress he would earn extra break time, free snacks, and eventually a day off (with his Father's permission of course). The one and a half years he was initially behind had dwindled to only 1 year behind with just over a semester remaining in the school year. He was making such great progress that some staff members wondered, just how did he end up at *The Program*. Staff members would say, "I wish we had more kids like Nelson, he is a great kid." That perspective changed shortly after *Craig-n'em* showed up.

*Craig-n'em* is slang for a group of dudes everyone knows are up to no-good. It is usually two or more immature decision-makers with a demeanor that depicts, "I aint gotta do nothing you say." I first noticed the change in Nelson after his return from the Christmas break. It started with the people he had chosen to associate with before the start of the school day. Initially he sat alone since he didn't know many of the students.

He was soon invited to sit with a group of kids that were known by the staff as a pretty good crew of academic achievers. They stayed off the no-break list, worked hard in the classroom and met their weekly goals. When *Craig-n'em* came to *The Program* it was as though a few bad apples were thrown into the bunch.

As a Counselor, I would observe patterns (academic and behavioral) to aide in developing an ongoing treatment plan. The plan identified objectives and goals directed at changing the behavior patterns that lead to negative outcomes. So, when I observed Nelson beginning to sit with *Craig-n'em* every morning before school, I knew where this was headed. It was reminiscent of the time that Sweetball joined ΣΦK. "Some people just don't need to hang out together," my grandmother would say. I discussed with Nelson while in a counseling session, the expression "eggs have no business dancing with stones," but he didn't want to hear it. He was allured by the fact that Craig-n'em would dress a certain way (pants sagging), talk back to teachers in class, and draw the attention of the students. Albeit, negative attention from the staff but adoration from the teenage girls in the program. He began to behave as though he needed to exert his manhood and do what my grandfather used to call, "Smelling-yourself."

Smelling-yourself is a dangerous mixture of being smart-mouthed, arrogant, prideful, stubborn, smug, and self-centered all rolled-up into the mind of an immature decision-maker. Nelson's new crew and the reactions of the teenage girls to his bad-boy image had his head and nose full of himself.

On this particular beautiful spring day all of the students, earning the privilege would be allowed to go outside. Although Nelson's new friends had earned the privilege, he did not. His behavior had become worse than that of *Craig-n'em* who had actually begun to improve. After a few one-on-one conversations and parent meetings about their behavior and their future with *The Program*, *Craig-n'em* soon chilled out.

The bell for the final period rang and students rushed to the foyer to read the list of names of students who had earned the privilege to go outside with their classmates.

Nelson's name was on the list of no-breakers. "Ahh Hell Nah!" he exclaimed. "I'm going outside, I like to see someone stop me," he proudly reported to his friends. *Craig-n'em*, no longer the ones drawing all of the negative attention, simply sat back and watched the Knuckle-head Nelson Show, as the staff used to call it.

The Program Director called the names of the students on the no-break list, instructing them to take course work with them into the no-break room. The students complied; however, Nelson had to put on his show. Arms waving, fists clinched, feet stomping, he began to rant "yall can't keep us from going outside. I'll knockout anybody trying to stop me," as he pushed chairs out of his way. That's when I got involved. "Nelson," I said calmly and assertively, "You've known this for two days now. We talked about this in my office.

"I told you that if you continued to misbehave and refuse to work in class you would lose the privilege to go outside. Now, you want to act like it is our fault that you cannot go out.......like we are keeping you from going outside, as if you are not accountable for your behavior? Dude, really?"

Nelson became enraged. His breathing became short, quick, and his eyes began to glare. He no longer looked at me but beyond me and toward the door. As his friends exited the building the sound of the door opening and closing began to overwhelm him. Each swing of the door allowed the sunlight to pierce into the foyer behind me. I blocked his path.

The rage inside of him soon boiled into fury. At that moment I was no longer an authority figure, but simply an object that blocked his path. An object that once moved would provide access to his peers. An object that once moved would display his strength and dominance over anyone that would prevent him from doing what he wanted to do.

He swung, and then attempted to push through me. I must admit that I am soft spoken; my tone of voice at times is very calming. However, my 6'5" 220lbs frame (then) was not easy to move, but it wasn't that. It was my Grandmother's lesson on the sincerity of expression. "Make eye contact, mean what you say, and say what you mean." As Nelson swung he knocked away my left arm. My right hand landed on his neck just above the Adam's Apple, thumb at the jawbone and fingers tightened. He was just as surprised by my reaction as I was sincere in my grip.

"Son, do not try me. Now, you still have a choice. You can relax and go into the no-break room or you can go outside for your few minutes with your friends after which you will be done here and you can return to your home school a failure."  I could see the fury in his eyes subside. He rested on his heels and I relaxed my grip. My hand moved to his shoulder, his eyes lowered, "I'm sorry," he said as he exhaled slowly and began to relax.

In that moment, I saw a flash of the time when I was Nelson's age 'smelling-myself' and chose to try my grandfather. Except, both my grandfather and I went flying over an ironing board and it wasn't his hand at my throat but the blade of his pocket knife. I said to Nelson, "Its ok, we're still good. Grab your work and go into the no-break room. I'll be in there shortly." As he walked away I walked to the counter, picked up the phone and called his father to report the altercation. "I'll be up there in a minute. Tell him not to get on the bus, I'm on my way" his father said.

An hour later the school bus pulled away from the building. Students on board who recognized Nelson's dad burst with both excitement and regret at missing the fireworks that would erupt once he confronted the Counselor who 'put his hands on' his son. Just as the door swung open the noise of a passing train exploded into the foyer announcing the angry parent. "What happened?" he exclaimed. With his son seated in front of us I recalled the details of the incident. He asked Nelson "is that what happened?" "Yes sir," he replied penitently.

I pointed out the daily behavior point average over the past two months. It documented a consistent decline along with a poor academic performance in the same time period. I explained the addition of *Craig-n'em* to the program and the affect it played in his son's downward spiral.

"You see, here we go again. I brought you here to get away from that last group you were hanging with. I told you they were no good and now you are back to making the same mistakes," his father barked as he stood over his son. Nelson stood, chest puffed, with intense emotion welled in his voice he barked back, "Well you made your mistakes. This is my life. Leave me alone and let me make mine." His father's face tightened and fists clenched as he inhaled and motioned toward his son. I interceded, placing my hand on Nelson's shoulder directing his gaze towards me. "That has to be the dumbest thing I have ever heard you say."

His father relaxed, appearing relieved that I had stepped between the two. Nelson's expression was now filled with bewilderment. I continued, "You are telling the man who wiped your butt daily long before you ever knew how.....and then taught you how to do it for yourself.....the man that held your hand so you could balance long enough to learn to walk on your own....and then picked you up when you fell so you could continue on....the man who fed you long before you could ever pronounce the word 'food'.....and still continues to provide for you.....the man who loved you so much that he is here now to beat my butt for putting hands on you..... Now you are telling him that you do not want his guidance, you do not want his advice? He only shared the fact that he has made mistakes in his life in the hope that it will help prevent you from making the same. You telling him to leave you alone and let you make your own mistakes is not only dumb, it is ungrateful!

"So what happens if he says ok, go make your own mistakes? Think about it like this: you wanted to go out and play with your friends, and walk around the block, right?" Still unsure of the point I was making, "Yes sir," he replied.

"What if you had never been around this block before? You had never strayed far from this building. Think of this building as your home and all that you know. The journey around the block is your road through life. In order to be successful, though, you have to make it around the block within a certain amount of time or the window for success will close. You, being headstrong and full of yourself want to burst through the door and take off running around the block because you are dead set on proving your manhood and that your elders do not know what they are talking about. But, I caution you before you exit, and say, 'Nelson, I've been around this block several times. I understand the trials that are out there.' Let me give you some guidance on how to make it around.

"First you will want to walk, not run. You can make it in plenty of time with patience and persistence. As you reach the first corner you will hear a lot of barking. There are dogs waiting and they will hear you long before you see them. Do not fear, do not stop and do not pick up a stick or anything to fend them off, because they are fenced in. It is just a lot of noise and if you stay to the left side of the road, away from the fence you will be fine. Now, the next trial is why you do not want to run. Just as you turn the corner on the left side of the road there is a huge hole in the ground. It gets dark on that corner and it can be difficult to see. So if you are not cautious and aware of what lies ahead, you will fall into the hole and it takes forever to get out. Ask anyone dealing with addiction. It is not a hole you want to ever fall in.

"After you make it past that obstacle you will want to pick up a little speed. There are a few logs stretched across the road but with a little speed you can jump over each of them. You can only go over, not around. There are huge ravines on either side of the road at that point and going around is not an option. So don't waste your time trying; it is just something you have to get over. Just as you get over that hurdle you will come upon a hill. It looks insurmountable, and midway up you will get tired. You will become weary and you will want to give up. But, I promise you that if you put forth determination, develop a desire to reach your goal, and remain persistent in your resolve....you will make it to the top. Just keep putting one foot in front of the other, keep moving and you will find yourself overcoming. And once you reach the crest you will see your goal ahead.

"On that final stretch ahead lives Sarah and her sisters. They are four of the most beautiful women to be seen. They call out to passersby from their porch. They will even encourage you to sit with them and drink a glass of cold refreshing lemonade after that tough climb. You will be tempted, but you must stay focused. Should you succumb you will find yourself sitting on their porch, resigned to a life of complacency, never achieving your initial goal. Time will pass you by and you will not even notice until the window for success has long closed.

"A journey is always most difficult closest to the end, and Sarah and her sisters will make it extremely hard to stay the course. So, do not be swayed young man, for the goal that awaits you is far more rewarding than a few moments of pleasure. The joy of accomplishing your journey is far more satisfying.

"You cannot make it around the block within the window of time needed to be successful, without the guidance of someone who has gone there before you. But with the guidance of others, using their wisdom, knowledge and experience, your journey to success can be as easy as a walk around the block. Now, by the expression on your face, you had no idea that all of that lies just around the corner."

Both Nelson and his father stood silent and pensive. "Don't refuse guidance, young man, especially from those who care about you," I added. "Patience, obedience and focused determination are ingredients essential to succeeding in the journey through life."

Nelson did well the rest of the year, very well. He reached his goal of leaving *The Program* with enough credit to be classified as a senior the following school year. A year later his father called to thank me. He said Nelson graduated high school and was accepted into a college

*The Evolution of Decision Making*

somewhere up north. He had family there and wanted to get out of the small country town for a while. His father recalled the day I shared the analogy of making it around the block. He spoke of how they talked about it and referred to it many times in the days after that meeting. That was my last conversation with his father. I hope Nelson has continued to seek his father's guidance as he travels around his block of life.

# Chapter 7
## Take a S.E.L.F., not a Selfie

Illustration 3

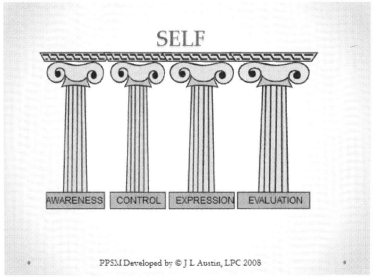

Awareness, Control, Expression, and Evaluation are the pillars in taking a S.E.L.F.

Taking a S.E.L.F is a moment when a person takes a Sincere Evaluation of their Life and Future. It is not a moment of vanity made famous by individuals whose sole purpose is self-promotion. It is an introspection of how your choices impact your present and your future.

Remember that moment, waking and sitting on the side of your bed? (Chapter 2) That brief reflection on the decisions that have brought you to a certain point in your life? That is what it means to take a S.E.L.F. Awareness, control, expression, and evaluation are the pillars that support S.E.L.F improvement.

**Awareness** – the key. Without increased awareness you remain in ignorance.

**Control** – the power to choose.

**Expression** – the action taken / a manifestation of your choice.

**Evaluation** – a judgment based upon the consequence of the action, you are either pleased/encouraged or disheartened/discouraged by your decision.

It is during the evaluation period when either the negative self-talk or the positive encouragement will direct your image of self, affecting your confidence in the ability to improve your circumstance by improving your decision making.

I first encounter the 6A while they are in the Evaluation phase of taking a S.E.L.F. In order to meet them where they are, I move backwards through the pillars. Because at this period in their lives they are not feeling too good about whomever they blame to be responsible for their circumstance.

## Self-evaluation
*You are not too happy with what is going on in your life now. You do not like the circumstances or the choices you*

*have made. You get angry, frustrated, depressed. You are not only mad at the world, but also with yourself. You hate that you have to deal with the consequence of your actions.*

## **Self-expression**
*You reflect on what you did or said that got you into this situation. Often asking, "Why did I do that, what was I thinking?" You think about what you should have said or done differently.*

## **Self-control**
*But, you let your emotions take control of you. You reacted out of anger, fear, depression, or simply out of spite. You were either unwilling or unable to control your emotions. Unwilling or unable to control your behavior and do what you know was the right thing to do. Or did you know?*

## **Self-awareness**
*Do you fully understand the capacity and range of your emotions? Are you aware of how you react to not gettitng what you want, or feeling disrespected? Are you aware of your emotional responsibility? Are you self-aware?*

Inevitably a time comes when you have to take a sincere look at how your choices have and will affect your life. In order to avoid most negative circumstances, awareness or the lack of awareness must first be acknowledged. Understanding and respecting that you may not know enough about a particular issue, topic, or about yourself, requires humility and a desire to learn.

These two characteristics, humility and the desire to learn, promote self-control.

Has there been a time that you needed additional information on a topic or person before making a decision? When you discovered the information, did it help in making the decision? You increased your awareness, which allows for more confidence in your decision. Then why not find out more about yourself? Why should someone else know more about you than you?

To the (6A) Adolescents: You do not have to live with mom, dad, sister, or brother the rest of your life, but you will have to live with yourself. Therefore, if you have to live with you, why not get to know, understand and love you? Loving yourself opens the door to your ability of truly loving others.

To the (6A) Adults: If you are still living with mom, dad, sister or brother as a result of your own poor decision making, shame on you; and in the words of *Outkast*, "you need to get-up get-out and get something. Don't spend all your time trying to get high.....cause you and I gotta do for you and I."

Do not sit around waiting for someone else to improve your life. Waiting for someone else to change what they are doing in order for your life to improve, is a change that may never come. Discover the power within yourself to better your life. As my grandmother used to say, "You better recognize!" Recognize that change starts with you.

**Self-Awareness** – The acknowledgement of one's emotional state, capacities, tendencies and limitations.
(Know yourself – Know your options)

**Self-Control** – The ability to control yourself and your behavior despite how you feel.
(The ability to choose)

**Self-Expression** – The observed behavior of one's emotions, or thoughts.
(Action taken)

**Self-Evaluation** – To examine, judge, or appraise some or all aspects of yourself.
(Consequential self-worth)

**Consequential self-worth** is the value an individual places upon himself/herself, based on the consequences of their decisions.

Many of the 6A expressed a belief that they could never improve their decision making. Low self-esteem and a history of poor decision making will cause a person to give up, and ask "What's the use? I am what they say I am, and I can never do better." I challenge that line of thinking by responding that life will hand you challenges, and there will always be people who doubt you and put you down, but you should not be one of them. Believe in yourself and soon others will believe in you as well.

Every man has his challenges. Whether he overcomes or comes undone is a matter of his choosing.

Be careful of putting your emotional health in the hands of others. Their thoughts and expressions about you are not the license to how you should feel about yourself. Your emotions belong to you. You have control of how you choose to feel about any given circumstance, situation, or consequence. You choose how you feel. No one makes you feel. The question "How does that make you feel?" places the responsibility of how you feel on some outside source. Simply asking "How do you feel about…...?" motivates the individual to search their own thoughts about the situation and accept responsibility for their emotion. You do not feel the way you do because of what happens. You feel the way you do because of your thoughts about what happened. If you do not like the feeling, change the thought.

*I am happy and content because I think I am.*
A.R. Lasage

Has there been a time in your life when your emotion got in the way? Have you felt angry while at work and unable to concentrate on the task in front of you? Have you found yourself grieving while in mixed company? How did you bypass the emotion to focus on what you are doing? Simply by changing your thoughts and saying to yourself (self-talk), "I cannot think about that right now." By changing the thought you increased your ability to concentrate on the task at hand.

> *Our minds can shape the way a thing will be because we act according to our expectations.*
> F. Fellini

Activity #5
**ANGER SCALE: IDENTIFY THE THOUGHT BEHIND THE EMOTION.** Participants in this exercise are asked to identify and define a specific range of emotions.

Activity #6
**STAN** Story telling is used to illustrate emotional responsibility and its effect on decision making. An illustration of negative thinking (self-talk) is brought to light as it progresses along the Anger Scale.

Activity #7
**Learning to cope in the moment.** Participants use examples given in Activity 5 to identify and apply coping statements. Emphasis is placed on their ability to change their world by changing the thought.

> *I am not afraid of storms, for I am learning how to sail my ship.*
> Louisa May Alcott

According to Edgar A. Guest you have all of the equipment you need for success. Here is an excerpt:

Jacques L. Austin

## Equipment

Figure it out for yourself, my lad,
You've all that the greatest of men have had,
Two arms, two hands, two legs, two eyes,
And a brain to use if you would be wise.
With this equipment they all began,
So start for the top and say "I can.".......
..................................
Courage must come from the soul within,
The man must furnish the will to win,
So figure it out for yourself, my lad,
You were born with all that the great have had,
With your equipment they all began.
Get hold of yourself, and say: "I can."

You can search the web for the poem in its entirety. Use verses from it and other positive quotations as part of your daily mantra. The messages that you repeatedly focus on about yourself, others, and the world around you shape your perspective. Learn to recognize what your current mantras are. Then shape, revise, or change them if necessary. Make the choice to see your life through a more positive lens. Here are two of my favorite mantras:

*Today is the beginning of a new day.*
*God has given me this day to use as I will.*
*I can waste it or use it for good.*
*What I do today is important, because I am exchanging a day of my life for it.*
*When tomorrow comes this day will be gone forever, leaving something I have traded for it.*
*I want it to be for gain, not loss; good not evil; success not failure; in order that I shall not regret the price I paid for it.*

---

*Everything will work to your advantage if you give it time to develop. Do not let self-doubts or negative thinking influence you to alter your agenda.*

## Chapter 8
## Discover Your Purpose

A few years ago I counseled a young adult who was both adjudicated and angry. He was in the stage of life where one struggles in search of meaning. He longed to discover his purpose. Of course this conclusion did not come easily. It was first expressed through resentment and disobedience at home. It was also expressed toward his friends and college professors who only sought to instruct their classes in the given topic. They could not help him understand the intense yearning within him for an answer to what he should do with his life.

His anger and confusion had shown its face while he walked along a crowded highway. He yelled and ranted at drivers who seemed to him to have an excess of "stuff." According to him, the only purpose to their lives was to gather expensive items (cars, watches, phones) and display arrogance toward those with less "stuff." His fury toward the unsuspecting drivers would lead to his arrest. He was soon released and eventually ordered to undergo anger management. Instead, he had come to the conclusion that he should take a walk-about.

A *walk-about* is an Australian Aborigine term that describes a spiritual journey males take during adolescence. It is an opportunity to commune with nature, search the soul, and discover a deeper sense of purpose. The young, angry, adjudicated, adult wanted to get away, much to the disagreement of his parents and the courts. He wanted to escape the trappings of the upper-middle class, and the expectations placed upon him by a greedy and vain society. He wanted to live on the land and the generosity of others. That is how he explained his plan to me. His bag was packed and he was ready to go. After an hour of venting his frustration about society he began to cool, and I responded, "It sounds to me like you're taking a S.E.L.F.; also, you want to know who you are and your purpose in life." In addition to The Evolution of Decision Making, I defined what it means to take a S.E.L.F.

Silence followed, then with a sense of revelation he replied, "You're right. I hear what everyone else wants me to do but I don't know. I don't know what I want to do with my life." I expressed to the young man that some people live their entire lives and never discover purpose. An easy guide to set you on the path to discovering your purpose is through patience, prayer, planning, preparation, and performance.

**The 5 P's to Purpose**

Discovering your purpose in life requires patience, prayer, planning, preparation, and performance. I explained to the young man that his purpose cannot be revealed overnight. It takes time.

**Patience** – Patience is essential to discovery. Even if you suddenly decide, with conviction, "I want to be a Navy S.E.A.L.," it will require patience. You may achieve your goal and complete seal training; however, attaining a goal may not reveal your purpose. The journey to your goal and beyond is revealing when discovering your purpose. Without patience the journey will end prematurely.

**Prayer** – My grandmother once told me, "A sincere desire is like a prayer. When you truly desire something of this world it is like the universe works in your favor to accomplish it." Believing, knowing that there is a higher power that works in your favor and will guide you to your purpose for living, allows for a perspective of success. Paulo Coelho wrote, "The Soul of the World is nourished by people's happiness and also by unhappiness, envy, and jealousy. To realize one's destiny is a person's only real obligation. All things are one. And, when you want something, the entire universe conspires in helping you to achieve it." You begin to understand that even the roadblocks and challenges along the way have meaning. There is a saying among believers: "The set-back is only a set-up for greater things to come." You have to Go-through in order to Grow-to what is meant for you. Patient prayer will make the journey to discovering your purpose richer.

**Plan** – Planning is the process of envisioning your success. Start a journal, write your plans down. The action of putting it in print reinforces your vision. The planning is all about thinking, and thinking influences the feeling. The more you focus your thoughts on achieving your goal, the more you will feel motivated to work, to study, and to prepare.

**Prepare** – Preparation is the action taken to achieve your goal. It is the days and nights of exercise, the long hours in the library, the leg-work to set up meetings, the applications that are submitted and the doors that are knocked on. It is the toil and the trials one must endure that will allow them to make the team, graduate the course, open the business, or get the job. A wise man once said, "It makes no sense to pray for a job but never fill out an application."

**Perform** – Performance occurs while you are in the position of the accomplished goal. You have opened the business, now it is time to manage it. You have made the team, now it is time to perform. Time to show yourself and others you are meant to be there. It is during the performance of your goal when either your purpose is revealed or you discover, "This is not for me." And if it is not for you, it is usually revealed early on. The effort in the preparation stage is dwindled by the idea of it not being what you really want. The preparation allows for the option to ask, "Is this what I really want, am I willing to put in the work required?" The journey to discovery can be profound. The motivation to get there must be fueled.

**Purpose** – When you are doing what you enjoy and you have worked hard to get there, you feel an appreciation that is unparalleled. You receive a sense of satisfaction like none other, and you understand its importance beyond yourself.......YOU HAVE DISCOVERED YOUR PURPOSE. Everyone has purpose, but unfortunately everyone will not discover their reason for being. Some decisions in life take individuals far from their purpose and many resign themselves to a place of complacency.

Do not become content with mediocrity. Become an intelligent decision-maker. Tap into your genius. Discover your purpose. And most importantly, DO NOT BECOME STUCK ON STUPID!

My conversation with the young, angry, adjudicated, adult that day ended after three hours, with his decision to go against the plan to take a walk-about. He decided he would attend the anger management groups as well as continue in his college education. "I guess I have to really work on that first P (patience), and there is no better time to start than the present," he said as we parted ways.

# Chapter 9
# Broken Glass

My wife and I were returning home one summer evening. The sun had just begun to set and as we entered the driveway we noticed it, a broken window pane in the living room window. I parked and walked onto the front porch. The window was double-paned. Between the broken glass and the intact inner pane sat a baseball-sized stone. I reached in, carefully retrieving the object and then showed it to my wife. She became infuriated. "Somebody's little knuckle-head child has thrown a rock into our window? You know, I saw those teenagers walking through the neighborhood recently, I bet you one of those pants-sagging-gangsta-wannabes did it," she stated emphatically. She was ready to hop back in the car and go look for them.

"This is a nice neighborhood. Now *Craig-n'em* come walking through and start destroying property. Get in, I'll call the police and let's go find their *lil' bad butts,*" she said as she reached for the car door. I began to laugh. She looked at me quizzically as if my laughter was directed toward her reaction. Well, partly it was. She was 38-hot, and ready for a confrontation. But primarily, my laughter was caused by a quick reflection into my childhood. "Karma," I responded. "Karma, what does karma have to do with this?" she asked. "What goes around comes around, and apparently it can come 30 years later," I said.

"Baby, kids will be kids. I did it when I was a child. Yes they were wrong, if they are the ones who did it. It's a window we can get fixed easily. We don't need to go looking for them. They'll probably walk through here again, I am sure I will see them. We do not need to get the police involved, I will say something." I tried to calm and assure her that the issue would be addressed. She responded, "Well, I hope you see them before I do. I am liable to let Stone loose on them." Stone was our 110 lbs. American Bulldog living in the garage. Very amiable with the family, he loathed strangers and would not hesitate to attack.

Then the quizzical expression returned to her face suddenly, as if I tried to sneak something past her. "And when were you throwing rocks at houses? You didn't tell me you ran with *Craig-n'em*." Actually I did know a dude named Craig who ended up taking a bullet in the butt trying to rob a bank, but that was long after the window incident. Anyway, one summer while visiting my grandparents, a childhood friend named Greg and I would venture off around the corner. You know, kids playing, exploring, looking for something to do. We were maybe seven or eight years old then.

We lived on the final block before an alley that was bordered by a fence with a huge growth of brush. There were houses on the alley-way facing the brush. Mr. Miller lived in one of those homes. He was a hard worker and understood the value in having your own. I would not realize that until later in life, but at the time we only knew him as the guy building his own home . . . by himself.

We walked by the structure several times on the way home or heading around the corner to Ms. Mary's house to purchase Bee-bops. One evening, close to sunset on the way home, we noticed a glimmer of light coming from Mr. Miller's home. The bare structure now had windows. It was lined with clear, unbroken glass that almost dared us and taunted our accuracy with the nearest stone. Who would be the first to break the glass soon turned into who will be the first to knock out the last piece of glass. We walked away feeling accomplished. We lay bragging claim to who had the greatest accuracy, or hardest throw.

The following day we started on our usual route around the block, not giving a second thought to the destruction of property the previous day. As we began to cross Mr. Miller's home, we noticed that the glare and sparkle from the new windows were gone and the piercing stare of an infuriated Mr. Miller peered through the empty pane. "Hey, you boys come here!" he belted out. We bolted. We figured we could make it to and inside of my grandparent's home long before he ever hit the corner. We made it to the house, but that was a different time in our society.

Neighbors knew each other and they knew whose kids belonged to whom. Soon after, there was a knock at the door. Mr. Miller stood at the door still angered as he told my grandfather of the damage to his home. I can still hear the roar of my grandfather's voice when he called my name that day. I can still see the fire in his eyes as he asked if I was the culprit, and the sting of his belt as a strike came with every syllable.

> 'YOU-KNOW-BET-TER-THAN-TO-TAKE-YOUR-BUTT-A-ROUND-THERE-AND-BREAK-THOSE-WIN-DOWS-I-BET-TER-NOT-EV-ER-CATCH-YOU-BREA-KING-A-NOTH-ER-PIECE-OF-GLASS-WIN-DOW-BOT-TEL-OR-NOTH-ING-YOU-HEAR-ME.'

On top of the sting from the belt, I was exhausted from running in a futile attempt to escape. Two weeks later when I was able to come out to play, I resigned myself to riding my green machine in little circles right in front of the house. I did not want to have anything to do with going around the corner. I did not care if Ms. Mary was giving away free Bee-bops. My butt stayed on 60$^{th}$ St."

My wife laughed. As we cleaned the porch she concluded, "Well it sounds like you learned your lesson the hard way." I smiled, "Yeah, it was a hard lesson; let's hope these kids do not have to learn the hard way."

I was on summer break from work. Life at *The Program* had become challenging. Years of facilitating anger management groups, individual and family counseling sessions, in addition to the private practice and responsibilities in the professional counseling association, I was spread thin. The respite during the summer was welcomed. Just a few weeks prior to the break I contemplated leaving *The Program*. I longed to work with another population. Teenagers can be emotionally and physically draining. I had begun to wonder if I was even making a difference in their lives. "Teenagers, they do not listen. I am just spinning my wheels, bumping my gums," was my mantra. I even questioned, "Is this what I am supposed to be doing with my life?" So I decided that while I was off I would search other work opportunities. Hopefully, something with adults again may become available. I learned some time ago that I could not lean on my own understanding, so I prayed. "Lord, show me what you want me to do, because I know anything you have planned for me is ten times better than what I plan for myself. Guide me in the direction you will have me go."

When I was not job searching, I passed the time by doing yard work and repairs to the home. My uncle used to say, "When you own a home, there is always something to do." Now I saw first-hand that he was correct. It was the first home that my wife and I purchased together. Working around the house was very cathartic for me. I would slip on my headphones and zone out to Frankie Beverly, Al Green or *OutKast*. Stone would often run around in the yard chasing the squirrels away while I worked; however, on that particular day he would serve another purpose.

I walked out of the garage onto the driveway when I noticed *Craig-n'em*. "Hey, you boys come here," I belted out and they bolted. Between my home and the neighbor's home was about 50 yards of brush. The neighbor had a fenced back yard with six dogs patrolling. I could always tell anytime someone walked down the street toward their home. Although I couldn't see them, I could hear the dogs barking, and as they moved on past the house the barking would subside, which I expected after the kids took off running down the street. I started heading back towards the garage when I noticed that the barking continued. I turned toward the street and walked again down the driveway. Although they were still out of sight, I could hear their steps heading back in my direction.

As I approached the edge of my driveway I saw one of them pick up a bottle and turn it upside down to empty its contents. As he came closer he began to pound the base of the bottle into his left hand. I began to size them up, because their decision to return had become apparent that it was not to talk. How would I explain a beat down by a group of teens in front of my own home?

In that moment I reflected on a military exercise where I was pitted against three attackers. My strategy then: attack first, attack hard. Take down the biggest one in as brutal a way as possible. The smaller ones would doubt their chances of survival and give up easily. When they came down the street toward me I could not determine any more about them than that they were a group of teen-aged boys. As they gathered in a semi-circle around me, their features became very distinctive.

There were four of them. The two younger teens, 15 or 16 years of age if I had to guess, were slender and unsure. I could see the hesitation on their faces, as if the idea to return was not theirs. They obviously were following the lead of the two older boys. The stature of the two younger boys was slightly smaller, 25 – 30 pounds lighter than the older two. They stood three paces away. The older teens both stood about three to four inches shorter than me. The one to my left wore a t-shirt with the sleeves cut off, his biceps tightened as he clenched his fists. He stood silent as if he awaited the command of their ring leader. The one to my right, the largest of them all, still with bottle in hand took a step toward me. With his head slightly tilted to his right, he surveyed me from head to toe. His facial expression appeared as though he had come across some foul odor. I could feel my heart racing. I rested my weight on my back foot, relaxed my shoulders, and just as I exhaled I felt a calm come over me . . . then I spoke.

"What up fellas? I came home the other day and saw that someone had thrown a rock into my . . ." "Yeah, so what?" The ring-leader cut me off. The scent of alcohol on his breath permeated the small space between us. Still maintaining my stance with arms by my side I observed the motions of each of them. I was expecting a sudden rush toward me. I continued. "I'm not saying you are the ones who did it." He interrupted again, pounding the bottle in his hand, "And what if we did?" It was becoming apparent he wanted me to be the first to throw a punch.

I expected at any second that Stone would burst from the garage, charging down the driveway and the boys would tuck tail and run. I peered over my shoulder back into the darkness of the open garage door. Stone was nowhere in sight. "I must have locked him in the pen," I thought. As quickly as I began to feel as though I was alone, my thoughts fell upon, "I will fear no evil, for thou art with me." I whispered a prayer (Lord speak through me), looked into their eyes and spoke with sincerity and clarity. "I am not mad at you. My wife, however, is pissed. But I explained to her I did the same thing when I was young, and I guess karma has finally caught-up with me." The ring leader exclaimed, "Man you got plenty of money, a big fancy house, why you worried about a window," as he now pointed the bottle toward my home. "Plenty of money, big fancy house?" I replied. "Dude, I am like every other adult, working hard every day to have something. The house looks fancy because I work to take care of it. I am out in the heat now working to take care of it, but this, this ain't nothing. I want more for myself and my family. I live in Lipscomb, a city in shambles. I would rather be in Helena or a neighborhood like Greystone (the more affluent areas). What I am saying young men, is that I have what I have because I appreciate and take care of it, but I strive for more, and you should want more for yourselves. Today you are throwing rocks, destroying property, drinking alcohol and threatening to jump on an adult. Come on man, really? Is that who you are? A bunch of drunk street thugs?"

The younger two looked at each other. The two older boys appeared startled that I knew they had been drinking. They relaxed their stare and took a step back. I stepped forward, directing my words at the younger boys. "You have got to be careful who you choose to follow. You may not see it now because you got that ignorant oil in you. But if you continue this same path, everything you hope to accomplish in life will never be achieved. Today you are drinking and destroying, tomorrow you are lying and stealing then next breaking and entering. You think the dudes who killed the family on Newhill started out that way?" I made reference to a murder in a neighboring community that occurred just weeks prior, where a family of four (husband, wife, and two sons ages 11 and 13) where executed and the home set ablaze in a drug deal gone bad. "No, they did not start out like they are today. But I bet you they will spend the rest of their days regretting their decision. An entire family murdered and set on fire."

"Look fellas," I said. Now holding their full attention I gestured as if I was a speaker in full control of his audience, making eye contact with each of them. "I am not saying you will turn out to be like those dudes, but when will the respect for others and their property begin? When do you decide to do what you know is the right thing to do? When do you appreciate what you have and work hard to earn more? When do you stop being followers and become leaders? When do you think about your future and how what you choose to do today will affect your lives tomorrow? When do you stop doing stupid stuff and start becoming intelligent young men? . . . Why not start today?" What happened next caught me by surprise.

The ring-leader lifted the bottle, turned, and threw it into the brush. He stepped towards me, reached out his hand for mine. As we shook, he stated, "I am sorry." I responded saying, "Thank you young man; do something with your life, do not become another imprisoned black man. Make better choices. Each of you, know this. Your life is the sum of all your choices….prisons are filled with people who made stupid decisions. Starting today, make intelligent decisions."

As they left the edge of my driveway they walked pensively down the street and past the barking dogs. The barking subsided as I entered my garage. I reflected on my desire to know if I made the right career choice. Should I continue to work with adolescents? Should I continue in anger management? Those questions were just answered.

"Thank you, Jesus," I whispered. Just then I noticed that Stone was not in his pen as I thought. He had become preoccupied with destroying an old comforter I planned to throw away. I smiled as I realized, everything and everyone has a purpose.

I returned to work that year with a renewed sense of excitement and focus. A strange phenomenon occurs when you discover purpose. The sky becomes clearer, the air becomes fresher, colors become more brilliant, the grass appears greener, and life in general becomes more joyful. That year I gave the first presentation on The Evolution of Decision making. We all have a purpose. What is yours?

The End

# Resources

Cook, John. *The Book of Positive Quotations*. 2nd Ed Minneapolis, MN: Fairview, 1997.

Eisen, Armand. *An Anthology of Black Folk Wit, Wisdom, and Sayings*. Kansas City: Andrews and McMeel, 1994.

T*he Holy Bible*, Authorized Version Set Forth in 1611 and Commonly Known as the King James Version. New York: American Bible Society, 1940.

Coelho, Paulo. *The Alchemist.* San Francisco: HarperSanFrancisco, 1993.

Caselman, Tonia. *Stop and Think: Impulse Control*. Chapin, SC: YouthLight, 2005.

Williams, Esther. *Breaking down the Wall of Anger*. Chapin, SC: YouthLight, 2000.

Beck, Judith S. *Cognitive Behavior Therapy: Basics and Beyond*. New York: Guilford, 2011.

Http://www.biography.com/news/famous-women-inventors-biography. *N.p., n.d. Web. August 20, 2015*

Jacques L. Austin

## Activities Index

*ACTIVITIES THAT TEACH THE EVOLUTION OF DECISION MAKING*

*Following is a brief description of each of the activities used to teach the Evolution of Decision making. The author recommends that the activities listed in this text be facilitated by a professional knowledgeable of the therapeutic techniques of Cognitive Behavioral Therapy.*

*Details and instructions on how to conduct the activities are available in Evolution of Decision Making: The Facilitators Guide, or by contacting the author for presentation.*

*Activity #1 THAT'S MY PERSPECTIVE, WHAT'S YOURS*
*Learning to identify automatic thoughts. In this exercise participants identify the nature of their perceptions, by bringing awareness to their automatic thought pattern and work to identify the thoughts that impedes change.*

*Activity #2 QUOTES – LEARNING TO THINK DIFFERENTLY*
*Using quotes from various cultures and regions, current thoughts and perspectives are challenged while learning to integrate a positive perspective.*

*Activity #3 A CHILDREN'S STORY*
*Story telling is used to illustrate the influences and effects of poor decision making.*

*Activity #4 EVODM*
*The decision types are reinforced through practical application. Each decision type is explored in personal context. Participants identify critical points in their decision making process that either promoted or prevented improved decision making.*

*Activity #5 ANGER SCALE-LEARNING TO IDENTIFY THE THOUGHT BEHIND THE EMOTION*
*Participants in this exercise are asked to identify and define a specific range of emotions. The group will then process their definitions and identify thoughts and physiological cues for each emotion. Emphasis is placed on their ability to incorporate coping mechanisms within the scale. Emotional responsibility is taught through this engaging and thought provoking exercise.*

*Activity #6 STAN*
*Story telling is used to illustrate emotional responsibility and its effect on decision making. An illustration of negative-thinking (self-talk) is brought to light as it progresses along the Anger Scale.*

*Activity #7 LEARNING HOW TO COPE IN THE MOMENT*
*Participants use their personal examples given in Activity 5, to identify and apply relative coping statements. Emphasis is placed on their ability to change their world by changing the thought.*

Jacques L. Austin

## **Acknowledgements**

March B. Perry and Elsie S. Perry for providing guidance and sharing the wisdom needed for my life journey.

Thank you, Dr. Jacalyn Tippey and Mrs. Philicia Witherspoon. Your assistance is without measure.

## About the Author

Therapist, speaker, and author, Jacques L. Austin is a Licensed Professional Counselor-Supervisor, and a Nationally Certified Counselor.

He is a member of the American Counseling Association as well as the Alabama Counseling Association, of which he has served in several positions as a member of its Executive Council.

Mr. Austin has extensive experience in working with the 6A (Angry, Abusive, Addicted, Adjudicated, Adult and Adolescent) population. He has been lauded for his ability to connect with the difficult client and offers a perspective for change that is relative and realistic.

He resides in Helena, Alabama and is available for consultation, presentation, and training.

aafcounseling@aol.com

Made in the USA
Columbia, SC
19 April 2021